PROBLEMS
?

PROBLEMS ?

REV TERRY MATTHEWS

XULON PRESS

Xulon Press
2301 Lucien Way #415
Maitland, FL 32751
407.339.4217
www.xulonpress.com

© 2019 by Rev Terry Matthews

All rights reserved solely by the author. The author guarantees all contents are original and do not infringe upon the legal rights of any other person or work. No part of this book may be reproduced in any form without the permission of the author. The views expressed in this book are not necessarily those of the publisher.

Unless otherwise indicated, Scripture quotations taken from the King James Version (KJV) – public domain.

Printed in the United States of America.

ISBN-13: 978-1-5456-6634-0

TABLE OF CONTENTS

Dedication ix

Introduction xi

Chapter 1—God's Problem 1

Chapter 2—Jesus's Problem 15

Chapter 3—The Church's Problem 23

Chapter 4—Our Problem 31

Chapter 5—Let's Be Real 47

Chapter 6 – Father : Son 53

About the Author 61

Note: All Bible references are quotations from the King James Version.

BOOKS OF THE BIBLE ABBREVIATIONS

Gen (Genesis), Ex (Exodus), Lev (Leviticus), Num (Numbers), Deut (Deuteronomy), Josh (Joshua), Judg (Judges), Sam (Samuel), Ki (Kings), Chron (Chronicles), Neh (Nehemiah), Psa (Psalms), Prov (Proverbs), (Song) Song of Solomon, Isa (Isaiah), Jer (Jeremiah), Ezek (Ezekiel), Lam (Lamentations), Zech (Zechariah), Matt (Matthew), Mar / Mk (Mark), Lk, (Luke), Jn (John), 1 Cor (1 Corinthians), Rom (Romans), Gal (Galatians), Eph (Ephesians), Phil (Philippians), Col (Colossians), Tim (Timothy),Tit (Titus), Heb (Hebrews), Pet (Peter), Rev (Revelation)

DEDICATION

This book is dedicated to my beautiful wife, Georgia, of over twenty-seven years; my four mothers, my father, Luke Matthews, my sons, "Terry Jr. and Lonnie" and also their mother, Carlene, who has since gone home to be with the Lord; to her God fearing sisters Gloria and Kathy, and to my God fearing in-laws; Eddie, Delores and Barbara; and to all my brothers and sisters [eight boys and three girls: eleven total].

To my biological mother, Louise Dupree Matthews, who went home to be with the Lord three days after I was born. The doctors told my father due to pregnancy complications that either my mother or I would die at birth. My father had to choose who he wanted the doctor to save. Although my father chose my mother, his wife, "God chose me." I'm not mad at you, Dad. After having eleven children, I would have done the same thing if I were you. Thank you, Mom, for sacrificing your life, so I might live. Doesn't that sound just like Jesus?

To my second foster mother, Missionary Evangelist Ethel Hines, who deserves all the credit for adopting me into the Royal family. She went home to be with the Lord a few years ago. You were a strong and dedicated woman of God. Thank you for baptizing me at the age of seven years old and allowing me to know the value of working in the church at such a young age, and teaching me that Jesus is the way.

To my third foster mother, Winnie Kennedy, who was a Sunday school teacher. You went home without my knowledge. I wish I could have been there Mom. I guess it wasn't meant to be. Thank you for teaching me the value of church attendance and the value of doing my school homework.

Finally, to my fourth mother, my mother-in-law, Aggie Black, who went home to be with the Lord on New Year's Day (the year is not important). Thank you for blessing me with your daughter Georgia. Mrs. Black you've got a lovely daughter. You continued to praise God unselfishly all the way up until your last day on earth. You're unbelievable, girl. I have never seen anyone do that before. Never! I heard you cry out "Thank You, Jesus," underneath your oxygen mask. You praised the Lord with your last breath. I will never forget you.

This book is also dedicated to all of the current and former members of Crown of Life Ministries. I love each and every one of you. As much as you say I inspire you to follow the Holy Lamb of God, you have "no idea" how much you inspire me.

Lord, "I thank you for putting these wonderful people in my life".

INTRODUCTION

One day while discussing the Bible with another minister, I was amazed that he seemed to disagree with me so vehemently. I was offended that he insisted on telling me his opinion on a certain scripture. I did not let him know how offended I was. He kept interrupting me and insisting I was wrong. He said I was misinterpreting a particular scripture. I disagreed with him entirely. He was older and had been pastoring longer than me, I think. I didn't want to argue with him, so I held my peace. After he left, I was angry with myself for not speaking up. Later, God told me that his version of that scriptural interpretation could be from a revelation he received, or maybe his interpretation was from the way he was taught. Whatever the case, my interpretation was clearly different than his.

Does God give different revelations to different people? I had other scriptures to support my interpretation, and he had his. Although his interpretation didn't make sense to me, mine appeared to be much clearer and more logical. I did not stop him and show him my scriptures. Due to personal time constraints at the moment, I was avoiding a long debate. I had too many things to do that day. However I would treat him to lunch one day so we could debate further. By doing this I could lay out my argument with my scriptures first. Then he could take it or leave it. By doing this, I would create food for thought in his mind. I would have planted a seed. Maybe someone else would water it. Eventually God would give the increase. If he missed the boat, then he missed the boat. Or maybe I'm the one missing the boat!

There are so many churches and pastors with different interpretations of the scriptures. This is one reason why we have so many churches and so many different ministers of the Word. We should all agree on the primary scriptures of the death, burial, and resurrection of Christ. However we tend to differ and have various viewpoints and interpretation of the secondary scriptures. Secondary scriptures would include anything outside of the death, burial, and the resurrection.

Whether we agree or not we should avoid arguing with our brothers and sisters for the simple reason of trying to convince everybody that we are right and everybody else is wrong. God may have given you revelations that He hasn't given to everybody else, and vice versa. One day you may see their point, and one day, they may see yours. Believers must learn to agree to disagree, and yet continue to love. Everybody is not going to have your same revelation.

CHAPTER 1
GOD'S PROBLEM

The entire Bible is a reflection of the Garden of Eden. This world in which we live in, is also a reflection of the perfect garden gone bad—very bad. God created Eden and chose Eden for man. He chose Eden for its' resources, it's food, it's water, and beauty. God is our resource, our food (bread of life), our water of life and represents our beauty of holiness. When God finished creating Eden and the rest of the world, He looked it over and said it was good. Even Satan was good in his original estate (Ezek 28:13-15)[1].

Trouble has no respect of persons. No one is exempt from problems, not even God. God could be exempt if He wanted to. He could simply program us to serve Him. No problem! God gets no pleasure out of forcing us to serve Him. Once sin entered into this world, God had serious problems. A world that was once "good" was no longer good. A world that was once sin free, was now contaminated. "God saw the wickedness of man was great in the earth and it repented the Lord that he made man. It grieved him at his heart" (Gen 6:5-7).

PROBLEMS?

Man's consistent and overt sins was the reason why God destroyed the world with the flood. Science has confirmed the flood by referencing the "ice age." Some parts of this world was frozen during the flood. However, the time frame of the ice age can be called into question. The flood represented the earth's original state. In the beginning when the earth was created, it was totally filled with water. It wasn't until the third day God said "..let the dry land appear" (Gen 1:2,9).

God has problems with His creation; man. So He decided to start all over. Man grieved Him at His heart. He chose Noah to assist Him in starting over (Gen 6:8). Noah was a just man, who pleased God in his walk. Noah found grace in the sight of God. When God flooded the earth, He saved Noah's family. Then God handpicked Noah's great grandson, Jacob (who God renamed Israel), six generations removed, to father His chosen people; the nation of Israel. When Israel became disobedient, God punished them by allowing a pagan nation (Egypt) to enslave them. [pagan = unbelievers] Eventually God rescued them from Egypts' house of bondage.

God had no problem getting Israel out of Egypt. His problem was getting Egypt out of Israel. Getting Egypt out of Israel continues to be God's problem today. Like the old saying, "you can take the man out of the country, but you can't take the country out of man." Sin works the same way. You can take man out of sin (jail/prison), but if you don't take sin out of the man, you've got the same problem. Many people who have been released from incarceration have returned to society in worse condition than they were before incarceration. It's a proven fact that prisons have created monsters. Without a doubt, prisons are well needed for shielding society from bad people. Protecting society is good, but what would be better is if the system could find the diamonds in the rough, and educate and train them to be better people in society upon their release.

Yes, God's biggest problem is, "us". Man was created in the very image of God, yet our behavior is contrary to His characteristics. God is good. Man is not good all the time. Man is sometimes evil. Man was designed to reflect God's image. Instead of reflecting the characteristics God, we tend to reflect just the opposite.

God's perfect creation of man is now birthed in a sinful state. We are born in sin and shaped in iniquity [wickedness] (Psa 51:5). Being born in sin doesn't mean we have to die in sin. Accepting the Lord into our hearts is our way out. However, although He's in our hearts, our flesh is constantly fighting against Him. The good news is that this is one fight we can win. In the midst of all of our shortcomings, let us focus on giving God His praise, so that we can be like Noah and find grace in the eyes of the Lord.

Another problem God has is, "Haters"! Psalm 81:15 says the haters of the Lord should submit themselves to Him. Romans 1:30 also makes reference to "haters of God". It doesn't matter how much good you do in life, haters will always be there. Haters can be a good thing. They will buffet you, lest you be exalted above measure. Haters will keep you humble. Also, haters can motivate you to prove them wrong. Let your haters be your motivators. Haters can slow you down but they can't stop you. Haters delayed the work of the construction of the Temple in Jerusalem; but the Temple eventually was built. The gates of Hell will not prevail against Gods' church. The kingdom of Heaven may suffer violence;

PROBLEMS?

and the violent (haters) will take whatever they can by force (Matt 11: 12). But what they don't understand is; the Kingdom of God is not flesh and blood; nor meat and drink. It's righteousness, peace and joy in the Holy Ghost (Romans 14:17). Tell your neighbor: "It's a spiritual thing"! The natural man cannot discern the things of the Spirit. It's foolishness to him (1 Corinthians 2:14).

Thou hast been in Eden the garden of God....!
(Ezekiel 28:13)[1]

Thou was perfect in thy ways from the day that thou was created, till iniquity was found in thee.
(Ezekiel 28:15)

And GOD saw that the wickedness of man was great in the earth, and that every imagination of the thoughts of his heart was only evil continually. And it repented the LORD that he had made man on the earth, and it grieved him at his heart. And the LORD said, I will destroy man whom I have created from the face of the earth; both man, and beast, and the creeping thing, and the fowls of the air; for it repented me that I have made them.
(Genesis 6:5-7)

But Noah found grace in the eyes of the LORD.
(Genesis 6:8)

Behold, I was shaped in iniquity; and in sin did my mother conceive me.   *(Psalm 51:5)*

---

[1] The book of Ezekiel references the prince and king of Tyre / Tyrus. God references Satan; the spirit inside of these men. Satan was in Eden. These men were not.

CHOICE

We only have two choices: God or Baal! We can sum up these choices into right or wrong; righteousness or unrighteousness, Heaven or Hell, good or bad, hot or cold, believers or unbelievers. Either you're a saint or you ain't. "Choose ye this day 'whom' you will serve." Baal represents all unbelievers. <u>This does not mean that all unbelievers are bad people</u>. Unfortunately, there are some <u>believers</u> who are not good people to be around. They are believers, with issues. (See Chapter 3) The Baal of the bible was an idol god. Satan does not care if you serve idols or not; as long as you don't believe, and serve the Almighty God through Jesus Christ. Because of God's great love for us (Eph 2:4); God gave man a choice. We can choose whether we want to serve Him or not. He wants us to serve Him simply out of a pure heart. "Blessed are the pure in heart for they shall see God" (Matt 5:8).

One of the reasons why God placed the tree of knowledge in the Garden of Eden was to see how much Adam loved Him. It's not known how long Adam walked around that tree before Eve convinced him to eat of it. We do know that Adam did not touch the tree until Satan devised a scheme to convince Eve to deceive Adam (1 Tim 2:14). Adam loved Eve also. Can you see his dilemma? How many times have we been there? Do we follow after what God says; or what ….says? God gave Adam and Eve a choice. He gave Adam the commission to <u>not</u> eat of the Tree of Knowledge. Why? Two reasons:

(1.) God was, and still is, our Tree of Knowledge; He is Omniscient (all knowing),

(2.) Love! God knew if Adam truly loved Him he would keep God's commandment (John 14:15). God would not get any satisfaction from forcing Adam to love Him, and honor His word. Likewise, God does not get any satisfaction forcing us to love Him and accept His word. If you could take a knife and cut God, he would bleed "Love".

Adam made the decision; the choice to defy God and obey Eve, his wife. This is a clear example of our spirit being willing and our flesh being weak (Matt 26:41).

Many people claim they love the Lord, yet refuse to keep His commandments. Why? Because the flesh is weak. Even though Adam knew He would suffer the consequence of death, he chose to disobey God anyway. He ate of the tree God instructed him not to eat of. Adam's spirit may have been willing to do the right thing, but his flesh was weak.

Adam was created in the very image of God. His Spirit was clearly capable to override his fleshly desire. Eve was the primary factor in Adam's decision (1 Tim 2:14). Eve heard a lie from Satan and passed that lie to Adam. Satan said, "ye shall not surely die." This lie caused Adam to reconsider the commission God gave to him. Satan knew he couldn't get to Adam directly. Adam was too strong. Adam was created by God, in the very image of God. Eve was created from flesh; Adam's flesh. Eve was bone of Adam's bone and flesh of Adam's flesh (Gen 2:23). Eve's flesh is what Satan appealed to. Satan knew he had a better chance of getting to Eve than Adam. Satan's ultimate goal was to defy God, and by deceiving Eve, she was to deceive Adam, thus defying God.

How many times have we given in to the opposite sex? How many times have we took our eyes off the Lord to focus on a fleshly desire and missed out on a blessing? The purpose of Jesus's coming was to give us strength lest we fall. But if we fall, He is our advocate. He is the "go between" us and God. Through Jesus we can ask for forgiveness and remain in good standing with the Master. However, we dare not frustrate the grace of God (Gal 2:21).

Contrary to God's word, Adam made a conscious decision to go against Gods' commission. He was tempted, drawn away by his lust and enticed [by Eve]. The tree of knowledge was pleasant to the eyes, and good for food, then lust conceived. Adam's flesh made the decision to fulfill itself; sin came forth, and entered into this world and death followed. The wages of sin is death.

Although Adam died at 930 years old; "a thousand years is as one day with the Lord" (2 Peter 3:8). What this means is; in Gods' eyes, Adam died the same day he ate of the tree. In addition, there is no record of Adam repenting for disobeying God. Instead, he immediately begins the blame game. Adam first begins to blame God for giving him Eve. He tells God, "that woman you gave me..." (Genesis 3:12). Then he goes on to blame Eve by saying, "She gave me [the fruit] of the tree, and I did eat." So Adam blames God and Eve; both at the same time. This is exactly how Satan works today. We blame everybody else for what we do wrong. It's never our fault.

We say things like "If he / she hadn't of done what they did, then I wouldn't have done what I did". This kind of thinking causes us to be easy prey for Satan. We give Satan a road map to know exactly where and what buttons to push.

Adam was convinced by what Satan told Eve, basically speaking, "God is a liar." God clearly told Adam "in the day thou eat of that tree you will surely die" and Satan [serpent] said "you will not surely die"thus making God a liar (Gen 2:17); (Gen 3:4). Satan is the father of lies (Jn 8:44). God doesn't like you calling him a liar.

In the book of Luke, when the priest Zacharias refused to believe Gabriel (God's angel), God immediately caused Zacharias to become mute. Zacharias could no longer speak (Lk 1:19, 20). He would open his mouth, but nothing came out. His refusal to believe God who cannot lie, insulted God. When God tells you something, and you refuse to believe it, you are calling God a liar. He is Truth and Life. Although God can do the impossible; there is one thing God cannot do: "lie" (Tit 1:2). God is the Father of Truth. Satan is the father of lies.

I could make the argument and say, "At the time God gave the commission to Adam, Eve was not created yet; therefore, she didn't know about God's commission to Adam." The problem with that argument is, Eve quoted God's words to Satan. Whether Adam told her or God Himself told her, Eve knew. Like Adam, she saw the tree was good for food (lust of the flesh) and pleasant to the eyes (lust of the eyes) and a tree to be desired to make one wise (the pride of life), and she did eat. How many know that misery loves company? She gave to her husband and he did eat. Again, Adam chose to make the decision to do what Eve desired of him instead of what God desired of him. The fact that Adam ate of the tree was not Eve's fault. Although Eve may have encouraged him; the decision was Adam's alone. Adam made the decision to disobey God.

The problem with choice is you can make the wrong decision. Salvation is not a guessing game. Adam willingly made a decision based on false information. So whose report are you going to believe? [Num 14:37; Isa 53:1; Rom 10:16]

Because God gives us "choice," we can choose who we want to serve (Josh 24:15; 1 Ki 18:21). Satan/Lucifer; who was God's former bright and morning star (Isa 14:12,13) had a choice also. Satan chose to be like God and attempted to deceive the world to follow after him instead of following after God. Since God gives us "choice" many of us "choose" not to serve our Creator. This unfortunate choice gives God problems, and it gives His followers problems also.

But God, who is rich in mercy, for his great love wherewith he loved us.   *(Ephesians 2:4)*

Blessed are the pure in heart: for they shall see God.   *(Matthew 5:8)*

And Adam was not deceived, but the woman being deceived was in the transgression.   *(1 Timothy 2:14)*

Watch and pray, that ye enter not into temptation:

the spirit indeed is willing, but the flesh is weak.
(Matthew 26:41)

I do not frustrate the grace of God...   (Galatians 2:21)

But, beloved, be not ignorant of this one thing, that one day is with the Lord as a thousand years, and a thousand years as one day.   (2 Peter 3:8)

But of the tree of the knowledge of good and evil, thou shalt not eat of it: for in the day that thou eat thereof thou shalt surely die.   (Genesis 2:17)

And the serpent said unto the woman, Ye shall not surely die.   (Genesis 3:4)

When he (Satan) speaketh a lie, he speaketh of his own: for he is a liar, and the father of it.   (John 8:44)

And the angel answering said unto him, I am Gabriel, that stand in the presence of God; and am sent to speak unto thee, and to shew thee these glad tidings. And, behold, thou shalt be dumb, and not able to speak, until the day that these things shall be performed, because thou believest not my words, which shall be fulfilled in their season.   (Luke 1:19-20)

In hope of eternal life, which God, that cannot lie, promised before the world began.   (Titus 1:2)

Even those men that did bring up the evil report upon the land, died by the plague before the LORD.   (Numbers 14:37)

Who hath believed our report? and to whom is the arm of the LORD revealed?   (Isaiah 53:1)

But they have not all obeyed the gospel. For Es-

aias saith, Lord, who hath believed our report?
(Romans 10:16)

And if it seem evil unto you to serve the LORD, choose you this day whom ye will serve. *(Joshua 24:15)*

How long halt ye between two opinions? if the LORD be God, follow him: but if Baal, then follow him...
(1 Kings 18:21)

And Adam said, This is now bone of my bones, and flesh of my flesh.... *(Genesis 2:23)*

How art thou fallen from heaven, O Lucifer, son of the morning! how art thou cut down to the ground, which didst weaken the nations! For thou hast said in thine heart, I will ascend into heaven, I will exalt my throne above the stars of God: I will sit also upon the mount of the congregation, in the sides of the north.
(Isaiah 14:12-13)

If ye love me keep my commandments. *(St John 14:15)*

DOES GOD LOVE US TOO MUCH?

Personally, I thank God for loving me too much. This is a benefit for us all. For God so loved the world He gave...! (Jn 3:16). Most people who are considered as "lovers" are also "givers". God's love for us is His biggest problem. He loves us unconditionally. The Bible says He loves us with an everlasting love (Jer 31:3). Because of His "great love" for us, He endures a tremendous amount of grief. The Bible says, "grieve not the Holy Spirit." We are constantly grieving Him either through our actions or our inactions. He absolutely loves us so much that He gives us an option to love Him back.

He loves us so much He gives us chance after chance after chance after chance. God is longsuffering toward us with the intent that "none of us" be lost and that "all men" be "saved" (2 Pet 3:9). This is a clear example of His mercy. His mercy endures forever (Psa 136:1). Many of us are alive today by the "mercies" of God. His Grace has been called the "unmerited favor of God." It's a "gift" from God. His grace allows us to obtain something we don't deserve. His Everlasting Love.

God's mercy is "not" getting what we "do" deserve (which is a good spanking). God is "Rich" in Mercy" (Ephesians 2:4). His mercy is a clear expression of his love. God does not have to put up with us like he does. He could end his pain of disappointment at any time. It grieves him every time we disappoint him. Because of his enduring love, he allows us to continue disappointing him over and over and over again, hoping that we will get it right one day. I'm so glad he loves us too much. Aren't you glad he loves us too much? Many of us should have been cut off a long time ago. We should continuously thank Him and praise Him for His enduring love.

LOVE HURTS

When you sincerely love someone, and they're constantly disappointing you, it hurts. If you were not acquainted with them, there wouldn't be as much pain or no pain at all. God knows each one of us. His love for us is so great that His grief may be even greater.

God's grief is so intensified He cried actual tears through Jeremiah his prophet. Later he commanded Jeremiah not to cry or pray for His people any longer (Jer 7:16, 11:14, and 14:11). God was finished pleading with His chosen people to return to Him. Too much hurt. Too much pain.

Mary wept over her brother Lazarus death. The Lord loved Mary so much and it grieved him so much to see Mary weeping, that Jesus began weeping. Yes, Jesus wept (Jn 11:35). Afterwards, the Lord immediately raised Lazarus from the dead. Oh the multitude of the tender mercies of God (Psa 51:1, 106:7, 69:16; Lam 3:32).

The Bible says love (charity) is patience, and kind, and long suffering. It envies not, it is not easily provoked. Love thinks no evil, and is not puffed up. Love rejoices not in iniquity, but rejoices in truth. It does not behave unseemly; it seeks not "her" own and most of all, Love never fails. May I add one more? Sometimes, love hurts!

For God so loved the world, that he gave his only begotten Son, that whosoever believeth in him should not perish, but have everlasting life.
(St John 3:16)

The LORD hath appeared of old unto me, saying, Yea, I have loved thee with an everlasting love: therefore with lovingkindness have I drawn thee.
(Jeremiah 31:3)

The Lord is not slack concerning his promise, as some men count slackness; but is longsuffering to us.., not willing that any should perish, but that all should come to repentance.
(2 Peter 3:9)

O give thanks unto the LORD; for he is good: for his mercy endureth forever. (Psalms 136:1)

Therefore pray not thou for this people, neither lift up cry nor prayer for them, neither make intercession to me: for I will not hear thee. (Jeremiah 7:16)

Therefore pray not thou for this people, neither lift up a cry or prayer for them: for I will not hear them in the time that they cry unto me for their trouble. (Jeremiah 11:14)

Then said the LORD unto me, Pray not for this people for their good. (Jeremiah 14:11)

Jesus wept. (John 11:35)

Have mercy upon me, O God, according to thy lovingkindness: according unto the multitude of thy tender mercies blot out my transgressions. (Psalm 51:1)

Hear me, O LORD; for thy lovingkindness is good: turn unto me according to the multitude of thy tender mercies. (Psalm 69:16)

Our fathers understood not thy wonders in Egypt; they remembered not the multitude of thy mercies. (Psalm 106:7)

But though he cause grief, yet will he have compassion according to the multitude of his mercies. (Lamentations 3:32)

But God, who is rich in mercy... (Ephesians 2:4)

...Yea, I have loved thee with an everlasting love... (Jeremiah 31:3)

Chapter 2
JESUS'S PROBLEMS

Jesus had problems also. His major problem was with the religious sect: the Pharisees and Sadducees. Can I say it like it really was? "Church folk". Yes, Jesus had problems with church folks. The chief priests and elders of the church hired lawyers and other biblical scholars to entangle Jesus in His words. The Bible says, "the chief priests and the scribes sought how they might take him by craft, and put him to death (Mk 14:1; Mk 11:18).

Jealousy is everywhere across the board. Whenever you impress upon people to take your product instead of someone else's; the competition will sometimes try to take you out. They will try to make their product better and/or attempt to promote a defect or deficiency in your product. The Bible says "jealousy is as cruel as the grave" (Song 8:6). It's a documented fact that many people are in the grave today, behind jealousy. There's even jealousy in the church. Pastors get jealous when another church is bigger than theirs. Choir members get jealous and say things like "Why does she/he get to lead all the songs"? Members get jealous and say "They seem to like him/her better than me", etc. Unfortunately, jealousy is part of life. God has reserved jealousy for Himself only. God's jealousy stems from serving Him and Him only and nobody else or nothing else. This is a righteous jealousy. If your children called someone else "Mama or Daddy" then you would feel the pain God feels. If your children praised or worshipped another man or woman in place of you; believe me, you'd feel the pain.

Once you are filled with the Holy Ghost, jealousy won't bother you. Because we're still human, it may creep up once in a while, but you won't react negatively to it. I've told people I was jealous of them as a compliment, which only caused me to strive to do better, so I could receive the same blessing. How many people know that your neighbor's blessing is your neighbor's blessing, and your blessing will be your blessing and yours only? It's coming. Just keep doing His will. It's on the way.

Once you get busy trying to handle and grow your business (church, ministry, etc.), you won't have time to focus on what others are doing. The Lord is saying, "don't bury your talent." Use what you've got. God gave one man five talents, another two talents, to another He gave only one talent. Use what God gave you.

The product Jesus was selling was "Truth and Life." The Pharisees and Sadducees were selling control, slavery and tradition. The religious sect of that time was selling Old Testament laws and the Ten Commandments. Jesus was selling fulfillment of those very same laws along with a new commandment (Jn 13:34). The people were buying it. The old religious sect was not. They were afraid that everybody would follow Jesus and put them out of business. The new commandment was "Love your neighbor as yourself." Love is an action word. Jesus was not selling destruction of the Law but fulfillment. What they didn't realize was Jesus was selling the same thing they were, but; it was new and improved. What they did not know was He, Jesus, was the fulfillment of the law. The law spoke of His coming; and He had arrived. The law was filled with God's words, and He was "The Word made flesh" (Jn 1:14). Jesus simply took the Ten Commandments and condensed them down to two: Love God; and Love your neighbor. On these two commandments hang all the Law(s) and the Prophets (Matt 22:40).

Jesus had another problem. Even His own family members didn't believe Him (Mk 6:3; Jn 7:5). His mother knew who He was. Jesus's brother James eventually believed in Him and became a follower. James is attributed to writing the book of James in the Bible. Jesus's mother never stopped believing in Him. At a wedding when she told Jesus they were out of wine, Jesus responded "What does that have to do with me?" His mother ignored him and told the servants "Whatever he tells you to do, just do it." This proves that Jesus's mother [Mary] obviously had witnessed a previous miracle before this first recorded miracle of the bible. Otherwise; how could she have known He was capable of this provision. Jesus then ordered the servants to fill six water pots full of water. He then turned that water into wine. Fine wine. The governor of the feast acknowledged that this wine was better than the wine that was served in the beginning of the feast. He accused them of saving the best for last. Normally they serve the best wine in the beginning and bring out the cheap wine last. This event was prophetic in the sense that Jesus was the last and best prophet of all previous prophets. The prophets before him were good, but none was better than Jesus Christ, not even John the Baptist, whom Jesus claimed to be the "greatest of them all" (Matt 11:11; Lk 7:28).

Another problem Jesus had besides His family was the Jewish sect [his peers]. He came among His own people (Jews), and His own received Him not (Jn 1:11). They did not believe that He was the Son of God. Just like in today's times. Despite the miracles Jesus did, many people refused to believe He was of God. He told them who He was, and He also showed them through his miracles, yet many people attributed the miracles to be of the power of Satan (Matt 12:24) and not from the power of God. Despite the doubters, many people did believe in Him (Jn 12:19). For this cause, many lies and false accusations were created about Him, which ultimately lead to His crucifixion.

Another problem that Jesus suffered, was homelessness. Many of us may never experience this. If we did, many of us would totally lose our minds. Can you believe it? There was a time when Jesus was homeless. He said, "foxes have holes and birds have nests, but the Son of man had nowhere to lay his head" (Matt 8:20; Lk 9:58).

Jesus's problems can easily be summarized into one major problem that exists today: convincing people that He was God. Jesus was left with no other choice but to come back from the dead. Why? Satan couldn't match that. Only God can raise the dead. Jesus said "no man takes my life unless I lay it down. I have the power to lay it down and the power to pick it up again" (John 10:18). After Jesus's crucifixion, the head officials paid the guards and soldiers to watch the tomb where they laid His body. Doesn't this sound like spiritual wickedness in high places? Doesn't this sound like corruption in the government? The bible says they were paid to lie and convince people that Jesus did not resurrect from the dead (Matt 28:12-15). Still today, many people believe that lie. Many believe that Jesus lived and died only. Millions do not believe "He resurrected" from the dead. Do you?

Once we become followers of Jesus, some of us may suffer rejection from some family members and friends. This is exactly what Jesus went through. Despite this suffering; the reward is much greater. This suffering is not worthy to be compared with the glory that the Lord will reveal to us and in us. (Rom 8:18)

After two days was the feast of the passover, ...and of the chief priests and the scribes sought how they might take him by craft, and put him to death.   *(Mark 14:1)*

And the scribes and chief priests heard it, and sought how they might destroy him: for they feared him, because all the people was astonished at his doctrine.   *(Mark 11:18)*

Set me as a seal upon thine heart, as a seal upon thine arm: for love is strong as death; jealousy is cruel as the grave.   *(Song of Solomon 8:6)*

Jesus saith unto him, I am the way, the truth, and the life: no man cometh unto the Father, but by me.
(John 14:6)

A new commandment I give unto you, That ye love one another; as I have loved you, that ye also love one another. *(John 13:34)*

And the Word was made flesh, and dwelt among us, (and we beheld his glory, the glory as of the only begotten of the Father,) full of grace and truth. (John 1:14)

Is not this the carpenter, the son of Mary, the brother of James, and Joses, and of Juda, and Simon? and are not his sisters here with us? And they were offended at him. *(Mark 6:3)*

For neither did his brethren believe in him. (John 7:5)

Verily I say unto you, Among them that are born of women there hath not risen a greater than John the Baptist: notwithstanding he that is least in the kingdom of heaven is greater than he.
(Matthew 11:11, Luke 7:28)

He came unto his own, and his own received him not.
(John 1:11)

But when the Pharisees heard it, they said, This fellow doth not cast out devils, but by Beelzebub the prince of the devils. *(Matthew 12:24)*

The Pharisees therefore said among themselves, Perceive ye how ye prevail nothing? behold, the world is gone after him. *(John 12:19)*

And when they were assembled with the elders, and had taken counsel, they gave large money unto the soldiers, Saying, Say ye, His disciples came by night, and stole him away while we slept. And if this come to the governor's ears, we will persuade him, and secure you. So they took the money, and did as they were taught: and this saying is commonly reported among the Jews until this day.   *(Matthew 28:12-15)*

CHAPTER 3
THE CHURCH'S PROBLEM

One of the major problems with the church is church folk. There are only two major types of church people: (A) Those who are "<u>in the church</u>," and (B) Those who have the "<u>church in them</u>".

Many people are "in the church," but how many have the "church on the inside of them?" There are more people in the "A" category than the "B" category. Churches are running over with "A-type" people.

Generally type-A personalities are most likely the aggressive types. They are the shakers and movers of society. Some are very educated and carnal minded, but they are very practical people. Sometimes this can be a good thing. They tend to get things done instead of just talking about it. The problem with many shakers and movers in church is when things don't go their way they tend to get upset and frustrated to the point they will upset and frustrate everybody else. This is not good.

The type-B people who have the "church in them" tend to be more laid back and demonstrate more faith in God. Because of this faith they tend to relax more, and they tend to let God do what He said He would do. This type of attitude can work counter-productive in the sense that nothing ever gets done. However, when it does get done, it will be right.

The type-A class can get too aggressive to the point they will drive people away. They tend to be more argumentative and more determined for everyone to see things the way they see it. Some "A" members come from previous churches. They can become very demanding because of the way they think things should be done. It's usually "their way or the highway." Either they will drive people away or they will quit. However, some of them refuse to quit or leave and will continue to hinder the church growth without knowing it.

The type-B class is your best class. Simply because when church is inside of you, you will consider other people feelings. Regardless of your opinions and or traditions, God's people become your major concern. Many traditions can stay in place but with an explanation and much consideration. Type-B people are the most considerate. The problem with the type B is they are taken advantage of many times. On many occasions their kindness is taken for granted and/or mistaken for weakness. Another problem with type-B people is they tend to procrastinate. They think they are waiting on God when the reality is, God is waiting on them.

People go to church for many different reasons. Some say "my parents went to this church," or "my family attends this church":

- "My girlfriend/boyfriend attends here."
- "They have so many activities."
- "It's for political reasons."
- "It's closer to my house."
- "They have a good choir."
- "They serve food after church.
- "They serve coffee in the mornings."
- "They paid my light bill."
- "They paid my rent."
- "They gave me a food basket…"

The list goes on and on and on and on! Don't get me wrong, these are all good reasons to attend and attract people to the church, but don't let it be the only reason! You don't want to do the right thing for the wrong reason.

It was Jesus's custom to attend church (Lk 4:16). We ought to make it our custom also. We ought to make going to church habitual; like going to work or like eating breakfast, lunch, or dinner. Church should be the spiritual food we need to eat every day and not just on the Sabbath.

Churches are constantly trying to find a way to motivate us and keep people motivated. God alone should be our motivation. For many, God is not enough. Again, try to avoid doing the right thing for the wrong reason.

DENOMINATIONALISM

The prisons are full of people from all denominations. There are Baptist, Church of Christ, Episcopalians , A.M.E. Lutherans; Catholics, Jehovah Witness, Methodist, Church of God, etc.; you name it; in there. They are not locked up because of their denomination. They're locked up because of "sin". Righteousness exalts a nation but sin is a reproach (shame) to any [all] people. (Proverbs 14:34) Even sinners don't like sin. They will break into your house but they don't want you to break into theirs. They will steal from you but they don't want you to steal from them.

The second and most major problem in the church is "denominationalism." First; I must say, denominations have proven be a "good thing" because it brings people of like-minded together in one place for praise, worship and learning. The problem is, many denominations think they're the "only ones" that are going to heaven. In the book of Revelation, the Apostle John saw a number that no man could number, of all people, all nations, kindreds, and tongues. They were wearing white robes. Somebody asked the question, "Who are these people?" John answered, "these are they who have washed their robes in the blood of the Lamb" (Rev 7:9-14). This is a clear indication that millions are going to make it into where the Lamb resides; from all walks of life.

The actual word "denomination" is not in the Bible. Denominations are formed because of the different interpretations of the Bible. For example, the Pentecostals say women shouldn't wear pants. The Baptists say it doesn't matter, yet many Baptist churches say women shouldn't be in the pulpit while another church has women preaching and pastoring. One denomination says, "the Bible says a woman shouldn't wear anything pertaining to a man"; yet another denomination would say "clothing stores sell women pants separate from men pants. The church has gone so far today as to approve openly confessed gay bishops. Homosexuality is no longer in the closet. They have admitted to currently living in this lifestyle and yet they continue to be promoted to higher offices in the church. This is a sure sign that we are living in the last days. Christians are now going in the closet while everyone else is coming out.

Another problem with the church is, many denominations will not fellowship with other denominations. Some denominations teach that you should "stay with your own," and "don't go to this church or that church." The problem with that is many of them believe in the same thing with minor administrative differences such as baptisms, communion, attire, economic differences, (rich, poor, good neighborhoods, bad neighborhoods, social status), etc. Denominations have separated us. Overall, churches are divided against themselves. Churches are fighting other churches. This is EXACTLY what Satan wants and what he loves the most. It's already difficult enough to live with God's people, even when everyone is supposedly on the same page. Look how many church people can't get along. God is not the author of confusion (1 Cor 14:33). He is the author of peace.

The contention among denominations has given people reasons not attend church at all. Research shows that a great majority of non-attendees do not go to church because their

PROBLEMS?

parents didn't go. They were not taught the value of church as children. This is why the Bible tells us to train up a child in the way they should go! This doesn't mean that this is the way they will go; however, living according to God's Word is truly the way all of us should go (Prov 22:6).

Many non-attendees don't go to church because they've been hurt by the church. There may have been a misunderstanding on somebody's' part. I hate to admit this but sometimes church folk will drive you away. I've seen it. The prisons are full of people who have been driven away from church. Unfortunately, there are some "mean" Christians out here. Some of the mean ones are hurt Christians. They don't intend to be mean. Many Christians need personality adjustments. The church is filled with hurt people. There are a lot of hurt people who are hurting other hurt people unintentionally.

Divorce and separation also play a major role in all this hurt and pain. Let's stop here and think: "If there are "mean people" in church; are they really "Christians", or are they a work-in-progress Christians? Only God knows, and time will tell. In the meantime, ask the Lord to help you to " bear one another's burdens" (Gal 6:2). If people are sincere about serving the Lord, they'll come around. Bear with them. Ask the Lord to give you strength to bear with them.

And he came to Nazareth, where he had been brought up: and, as his custom was, he went into the synagogue on the Sabbath day...!   *(Luke 4:16)*

For God is not the author of confusion, but of peace, as in all churches of the saints.
(1 Corinthians 14:33)

Train up a child in the way he should go...
(Proverbs 22:6)

Bear ye one another burdens, and so fulfill the law of Christ. *(Galatians 6:2)*

CHAPTER 4
OUR PROBLEM

Time will not allow for our problems to be fully explained. Our problems are vast. It may take an entire book or up to five, maybe ten additional books to explain. Libraries are filled with solutions to our problems. Self-help books are flying off the shelves. From yoga books to child development books to mind control books to hypnosis. Our society is obsessed with making ourselves better or finding ways to help us to understand why we do what we do and feel what we feel. There are many factors that shape our personalities: social, economic, geographical, environmental, psychological, physiological, emotional, mental, educational, intellectual, marriage, divorce, injuries, our childhood, and on and on! These all play a role in shaping who we are; including absent fathers, absent mothers, abusive parents, alcoholic parents, educated and uneducated parents, or no parents at all. The list goes on and on!

Despite these factors, one factor is common among us all: God! Either He's in our life or He's not. Whether we believe in Him or not, God is the Creator of us all (Eph 4:6). At some point in time, we should recognize this. Some do and some don't, and some don't care. God is the creator of us all, is in us all, and works through us all, whether we accept Him or not. We need the Lord to survive.

Because God is the creator of all, despite the environment we are born into, our problems appear to allude to one major factor—spiritual. Our problems are more spiritual than natural. We can't overlook the child born into an impoverished home or impoverished country. Many children have natural needs that have not been met, and therefore cannot concentrate on spiritual needs. Their natural deficiencies (their handicap, sickness, hunger, etc.) will not allow them to see beyond their next meal.

This book is designed toward anyone who is competent to make a decision to either follow or reject the Lord. Despite our childhood deficiencies, whether they are voluntary or involuntary, parents are held responsible in the eyes of God to train up a child in the way they should go. Many parents don't do this simply because: (1) they were not raised / taught as a child about the Lord; (2) somewhere in time they made the decision not to accept the Lord. Many parents were raised with the understanding of placing little or no value on finding the Lord, thus their children are raised the same way. According to the Bible, before the end of time, "The gospel shall be preached in all nations, and then shall the end come" (Matt 24:14). And before it's all over, every knee shall bow and every tongue will confess that Jesus Christ is Lord of all; (Rom 14:11)

God is our creator, and we need Him to survive. When doctors get sick, they need a doctor. Lawyers sometimes need a lawyer themselves. Judges need judges. Teachers had a teacher, at one time, to teach them. Accountants learned from other accountants, etc. We all need each other at some point in time. To buy a house, in most cases, a realtor is involved; escrow is opened; someone does a title search to secure the title, and someone else records the title. Someone had to find the land, purchase the land, and maybe develop the land. Someone laid the foundation brick by brick. Someone else had to run the water lines, electrical lines, phone lines, build and/or dig a well if needed, etc. Just like in the construction of a home that needs carpenters, welders, architects, engineers, brick layers, plumbers, and electricians, etc., God fixed it that we all need each other to survive.

Some of us recognize that we need the Lord to survive, and yet many others don't. It appears like there are more people that do not recognize the Lord than do. Some just outright reject the Creator. Some people have laid claim to being an agnostic; in other words, they don't know if there is a God, and don't care.

ATHEISM

There will come a time when men will not endure sound doctrine. *2 Timothy 4:3*

Atheists reject God. They don't believe in God. The problem with atheism is "even Satan believes in God" (James 2:19). Many people have laid claim to being an atheist. Satan has tricked them. Yes, Satan has fooled them (Psa 14:1, 53:1).

Satan has tricked the minds of the unbeliever when Satan himself is a believer. What is even worse, despite their denial of God; God cannot deny Himself (2 Tim 2:13). Atheists don't realize that the air they breathe belongs to God. The very breath they use to deny His existence belongs to God. So where do they get the audacity to deny Him? The Bible has a special name for these special people in Psalm 14 and Psalm 53. How can one escape if they neglect so great salvation? (Heb 2:3). In God we live, we move, and have our being (Acts 17:28). Somehow a portion of God's creation has been convinced that they operate on their own power. Ironically, some have given credit to a higher power, not realizing that this higher power is God Himself.

FAITH

Another major problem with most of us, is our faith. Most of us have faith in everything but God. We have more faith in our cars, our jobs, in people, family, friends, and even ourselves than we do in God. The faith problem applies to both believers and unbelievers.

Let's begin with the believers. Many believers have problems focusing. They have faith in God, but many believers lose focus when problems take center stage. What we fail to understand is that the Lord should be center stage. Every believer has been guilty of this. We may not want to admit it, but we have all been there.

Once our problems become our main focus; the Lord takes a back seat to our thought process; to our solution. The Bible says, "He will keep us in perfect peace whose mind is stayed on him" (Isa 26:3). Unfortunately, the option of focusing on the Lord is usually executed after we've exhausted everything else. We tend to forget to put God first, and let Him lead you to the solution. Question: How do we put him first? Answer: Pray without ceasing (1 Thess 5:17). It begins when we first wake up in the morning. Start praying to Him immediately and thanking Him for another day. He will take care of the rest of your day. He will help you throughout your day. "Seek ye first the Kingdom of God and his righteousness and all the other things will be added unto you" (Matt 6:33).

Even believers lose faith in God from time to time, while unbelievers never had faith. We've all been there. Some are there right now. Some unbelievers had it at one time, and because God didn't react the way they expected Him to react and do what they expected Him to do, they became angry with God. They ask questions like: "If there's a God then why….?" Why didn't God prevent this (or that) from happening? They also say things like, "If God is so good, then why do bad things happen to good people?" One answer to that is Satan! Satan is busy trying to discourage us. He's pretty good at his job. Satan does these things, so you can get mad at God. He does these things so you can stop praying, stop believing, stop serving, and stop focusing on what God has called you to do. Don't let him get the victory. We need to be like "Job" in the bible. In all the things that Satan did to him, he never sinned nor charged God foolishly (Job 1:22).

Regardless of what Satan does, we must keep putting our faith and trust in God. We need to stop blaming God for everything that goes wrong. Start blaming Satan. Satan is the one that comes to rob, kill, and destroy (Jn 10:10). Jesus comes so that we will have life and life more abundantly". Every good gift and perfect gift comes from God (James 1:17). Sometimes we sound like we're trying to tell God what He is supposed to do? Ask yourself, Am I doing everything I'm supposed to do? It's a true life lesson that; bad things happen to good people. Bad things have been happening to good people from the beginning of time. After Adam disobeyed God, sin entered into this world. Sin is still here, and it's here to stay until Jesus returns. Bad things didn't just start after you were born. Nobody has the full explanation for this, except God. When bad things happen it seems like everybody gets mad at God. At the time we need God most many people will blame God and pull away from Him instead of drawing closer to the only source that can fix it.

Some people will say, "God allowed these bad things to happen." When you're in Christ many of these bad things happen for our good. We just don't see it. For believers, all things work together for good to them who love the Lord! (Romans 8:28). "All things" means just that; silly things, stupid things, dumb things, crazy things, horrible things, illness, accidents, etc., etc. We have to ask God to show us the message in the mess. Some messages are revealed immediately, and some we'll understand better by and by. One thing for sure, it won't be right until we get to Heaven. Let Heaven be your goal. Satan can't touch you up there. This earth is Satans' domain. He is the prince of the air. (Ephesians 2:2) (see Chapter 5)

Our problem is twofold: (1) unbelievers don't have faith in God for whatever reason; (2) believers have faith, but sometimes their faith wavers. Not good. There are circumstances that arise in life that causes your strongest believers to doubt God. This wavering of faith exists among both the believers and the unbelievers. Quiet as it is kept, sometimes unbelievers will experience more faith in their "higher power" than believers do in God. God wants us to have un-yielding faith that will not buckle under any circumstances. This is why Paul said on his death bed, "I've fought the good fight, and I kept the faith" (2Tim 4:7). If anyone had a reason to doubt God, Paul and Job did. Job said, "Though He (God) slay me, yet will I trust Him" (Job 13:15). The Bible says, "Without faith it's impossible to please God" (Heb 11:6). Believers struggle with it while unbelievers lack it entirely.

Many believers tend to lose faith periodically, for whatever reason, and then find it later. Some believers are weak in faith. Even Jesus's followers (apostles) asked Him to increase their faith (Lk 17:5). Some have great faith, and some have little faith. God has given to every one of us a measure of faith (Rom 12:3). With this measure we are to feed it, and allow it to grow. How do we feed it? We work it. We pray without ceasing. We don't pray enough. Working your faith is relative to your prayer life. How do we work your faith? How do we exercise your faith? By increasing your prayer life. If your prayer life is consistent, then you are consistently depending and believing on God to bring you through. True faith is not about everything turning out okay. True faith is being okay, no matter how things turn out.

Faith without works is dead. Speak faith, and act on it as God instructs you. Many times we curl up and do nothing. Do something. Whatever you do, don't stop. Keep it moving. Don't draw back in fear. God has no pleasure in a drawback spirit (Heb 10:38). The problem is many believers still doubt God about certain things. Yes, even believers find it difficult to place ALL of our trust in Him.

Another one of our problems stems from what happens between Sundays. From one Sunday to the next, things happen. These "things" are what discourages us and cause us to weaken our faith. These "things" are what we call, "life". Life happens.

TRIALS AND TRIBULATIONS

Everybody wants to make you think their life is not as bad as it really is. Facebook is one of the most popular tools we use to inform the world that our lives are peachy wonderful. There are some who use Facebook to express their pain, and some use it to lash out. Overall, Facebook is filled with mostly smiles and happy times. This is good. However; in reality, many of them that are smiling on the outside are crying on the inside. Sometimes we smile to keep from crying. I've seen people smile and cry at the same time. They tried to put on the face of joy, but the tears of pain prevail.

Everyone experiences trials and tribulation: no one is exempt. If you have not experienced a trial, just keep living. A trial comes when your faith is tested. Some of us pass, and some of us fail. Trials are composed of short periodic tests.

They are little episodes that stem from making good or bad decisions. A tribulation can be what happens as the result of a bad decision. Tribulations are more long term. Tribulations can also come without any provocation. Either way, our faith is tested. Tribulations could be financial, health issues, family issues, marital issues, problems in the work place, problems with other people, etc. Death of a family member or a close friend can trigger a tribulation. Tribulations can take on a life of their own. They can seem to be never-ending. All of these could lead to depression, stress, persecutions, etc. Tribulations can also be summed up as just plain trouble. The Bible says, "All that live godly...shall suffer persecution (2 Tim 3:12). Paul said, "We are troubled on every side" (2 Cor 4:8). Jesus said "In this world we shall have tribulation..." (Jn 16:33). However, Jesus also assures us in that same passage, "Be of good cheer, (because) I have overcome the world." Isn't this the side you want to be on? On the side of the Overcomer? Of course you do! Everybody does!

Our problems can be summed up into this. There are only two kinds of people in this entire world: believers and unbelievers. We've discussed some of the problems with believers. The other problem with believers is there are so many different beliefs. There are so many different interpretations of the Bible. There are different doctrines and administrations but the same Lord. There are diversities of operations, but it is the same God which works all in all (1 Cor 12:5,6). Despite our differences, if we are serving the same God, then we must learn to agree to disagree. If we are not serving the same God, sin lies at the door (Gen 4:7). There is only one God (Eph 4:5); One Lord, One faith, and One baptism.

Although unbelievers live on the same earth, they are in a different world. When two unbelievers clash, the results are disastrous and sometimes fatal. Believers must find a way to follow peace with all men; otherwise, none of us are going see Heaven (Heb 12:14). If we can't get along down here, why would God want us up there? Remember two (2) crucial words that will help us along this journey of life: Patience and Respect. When we have patience with people and respect everyone, you will see our stress level decrease. May patience possess ye your souls (Lk 21:19). Having patience with people can sometimes be very difficult. Remember God had patience with us. In addition, some people seem not to deserve the respect you give them. Some don't return it; either out of ignorance or just outright rudeness. Many will try your patience until you feel like you're about to explode. Ask the Lord to increase your faith and to increase your patience (Lk 17:5). God will answer your request. Also, remember that the Lord will not put more on you than you can bear (1 Cor 10:13).

For in him we live, and move, and have our being...!
(Acts 17:28)

And this gospel of the kingdom shall be preached in all the world for a witness unto all nations; and then shall the end come.   (Matthew 24:14)

Thou believest that there is one God; thou does well: the devils also believe, and tremble.   (James 2:19)

The fool hath said in his heart, There is no God.   (Psalm 14:1, Psalm 53:1)

If we believe not, yet he abides faithful: <u>he cannot deny himself</u>. *(2 Timothy 2:13)*

How shall we escape, if we neglect so great salvation…! *(Hebrews 2:3)*

Thou wilt keep him in perfect peace, whose mind is stayed on thee: because he trusted in thee. *(Isaiah 26:3)*

Pray without ceasing. *(1 Thessalonians 5:17)*

Seek ye first the kingdom of God, and his righteousness; and all these things shall be added unto you. *(Matthew 6:33)*

In all this Job sinned not, nor charged God foolishly *(Job 1:22)*

The thief cometh not, but for to steal, and to kill, and to destroy: I am come that they might have life, and that they might have it more abundantly. *(John 10:10)*

Every good gift and every perfect gift is from above, and cometh down from the Father of lights, with whom is no variableness, neither shadow of turning. *(James 1:17)*

I have fought the good fight, I have finished my course, I have kept the faith. *(2 Timothy 4:7)*

Though he slay me, yet will I trust in him:…! (Job 13:15)

But without faith it is impossible to please him: for he that cometh to God must believe that he is! *(Hebrews 11:6)*

And the apostles said unto the Lord, increase our faith.
(Luke 17:5)

God hath dealt to every man the measure of faith.
(Romans 12:3)

Now the just shall live by faith: but if any man "draw back", my soul shall have no pleasure in him.
(Hebrews 10:38)

All that will live godly in Christ Jesus shall suffer persecution. (2 Timothy 3:12)

We are troubled on every side, yet not distressed; we are perplexed, but not in despair. (2 Corinthians 4:8)

These things I have spoken unto you, that in me ye might have peace. In the world ye shall have tribulation: but be of good cheer; I have overcome the world.
(John 16:33)

There are differences of administrations, but the same Lord. There are diversities of operations, but it is the same God which worked all in all.
(1 Corinthians 12:5-6)

If thou does well, shalt thou not be accepted? and if thou does not well, sin lies at the door...! (Genesis 4:7)

Follow peace with all men, and holiness, without which no man shall see the Lord. (Hebrews 12:14)

In your patience possess ye your souls. (Luke 21:19)

There hath no temptation taken you but such as is common to man: but God is faithful, who will not suffer you to be tempted above that ye are able; but will with the temptation also make a way to escape, that ye may be able to bear it. *(1 Corinthians 10:13)*

Wherein in time past ye walked according to the course of this world, according to the prince of the power of the air, the spirit that now works in the children of disobedience: *(Ephesians 2:2)*

SIN OF OMISSION

Therefore to him that knows to do good, and does it not; to him it is sin. —James 4:17

The major problem among believers is that many times they fail to do the right thing when the opportunity presents itself. God puts us in a position where He can use us most, and we freeze. We freeze because we are scared of (a) what people may say, or (b) we begin to think God might not show up. What we fail to see is God is already in us. God is going to do what He's going to do, regardless. Working our faith opens the door for God to go to work immediately. How do we work our faith? We call those things which be not as though they were (Rom 4:17). In other words; we name it and claim it. While Jesus was standing at the gravesite of Lazarus, He looked up to Heaven and said, "Lazarus, come forth!" Before Lazarus arose, Jesus called him to come forth (Jn 11:43). By calling Lazarus to "come forth," Jesus was calling those things which be not (Lazarus was dead) as though they were (Lazarus arose). Jesus did this for two reasons: (1) "He loved Lazarus" (Jn 11:5, 36), and (2) to increase the faith of those who witnessed this resurrection (Jn 11:42). [Because of the people standing by ... that they may believe that God had sent Him.]

Raising a dead man from the grave presented "another opportunity" to the non-believers who doubted Jesus as being the Son of God. Surely if this didn't convince them, what else could He do? Raise himself from the dead? Hello?

When we fail to do the right thing, we grieve God. To him that knows to do and does not, it is sin (James 4:17). This sin has been labeled as the sin of omission. When you omit to do the right thing, it's considered a sin. Many people think sin is an "act" only. Sin is also refusing to act. You can commit sin with a sinful act, and you can be guilty of omitting to do the right thing, thus sinning by omission. Many Christians say, " I don't want to get involved." By doing this they think they can't be accused of doing anything wrong. The Lord will tell you when it's time to get involved. When you refuse to act on the Lord's behalf, you become just as guilty as the person committing a sin, simply by omission or failing to do the right thing. Then what is your purpose of being here? How can God use you if you don't respond to the call? A fireman defies his purpose if he willfully refuses to put a fire out. If he attempts to put the fire out, and he doesn't succeed, at least we can say he tried. All you have to do is take a first step. God will do the rest.

And when he thus had spoken, he cried with a loud voice, Lazarus come forth. *(John 11:43)*

And I knew that thou hearest me always: but because of the people which stand by I said it, that they may believe that thou hast sent me. *(John 11:42)*

Now Jesus loved Martha, and her sister, and Lazarus. *(John 11:5)*

Then said the Jews, Behold how he loved him! *(John 11:36)*

Therefore to him that knows to do good, and doeth it not, to him it is sin. *(James 4:17)*

Every good gift and every perfect gift is from above, and cometh down from the Father of lights! *(James 1:17)*

CHAPTER 5
LET'S BE REAL

LUKE 4:5,6

Jesus allows Satan to take Him to a high mountain. Satan shows Him all the kingdoms of the world. Then Satan tells Jesus, "All this power will I give you...for that is delivered unto me." Let's stop right here! "Delivered unto me." I repeat: "delivered unto me." Ditto: "delivered unto me"? Satan admits that somebody <u>delivered</u> "all the kingdoms of the world" to him. Who else can deliver kingdoms, other than the one who created them? Nobody but God could do this!

Satan who is the father of lies cannot lie about the creation of the world. Even Satan had to honor this truth. He knows that he did not create the world nor the kingdoms in it. If Satan created the world then he could take credit for creating God. God is the creator of Heaven and Earth; and Satan knows this and cannot refute it. Even Satan knows God created him.

God delivered the kingdoms to Satan! God delivered "earth" to Satan with the intention that Satan would do the right thing. Satan was God's most beautiful angel (cherub) (Ezek 28:13-17). Even Satan admits that the kingdoms were given/delivered to him. His true purpose for admitting this was to inform Jesus that he (Satan) was in charge of these kingdoms and by being in charge of something that God gave him also granted him the power to give it to whomever he chooses. Yes, Satan was given the power to give these kingdoms to whomsoever he so desires (with God's permission of course). Satan's only reason for telling Jesus this truth was to deceive Jesus. When Satan lies, his intent is to deceive, and when he tells the truth, his intent is the same. He is the father of deception.

Did Satan know that Jesus was the Son of God? If so, then why did Satan challenge Jesus's Son-ship? Was it because Jesus was now "in the flesh"? Satan was hoping that Jesus's flesh would seize on this opportunity to defy His Father, God. This is what Satan does. This defiant behavior is what caused Satan to be cast out of Heaven in the first place (Isa 14:12; Lk 10:18). Satan was looking for a partner in crime. If Satan could convince Jesus, who the bible refers to as the "last Adam" (1 Cor 15:45, 47) to defy God like he convinced the "first Adam"; this would score a major victory for him.

While tempting Jesus, Satan says, "IF." "If you be the son of God..." Did Satan think that because God, who was now made flesh, would give in to the desires of the flesh? The flesh is weak, but the spirit is willing (Matt 26:41). Satan knows that the flesh is weak. This is why the Bible tells us to walk in the Spirit (of God), and God will give you the power to resist the lust of the flesh (Gal 5:16,17).

Satan was given this power to rule over earth! God gives His angels to keep "charge over us, lest we dash one foot against a stone" (Psa 91:11-12). God assigns His angels to watch over us, all night and all day. Does anybody remember the song,"All night, all day, the angels watching over me my Lord"? The Bible refers to the serpent (Satan) as being "subtle" [wise or keen] (Gen 3:1). God chose him because of his wisdom and his wit. He was also beautiful (Ezek 28:13, 17). Musical instruments were built into his wings (Ezek 28:13). Because of these instruments many have said he was the head of the Heavenly choir. Some have said he was in charge of the Heavenly host [army of angels]. He may have been an "orchestra" all by himself. He excelled over all the other angels God created. Satan's assignment: Earth, "the Holy Mountain of God (Ezek 28:14 and Zech 8:3)

Who gave Satan this power? God! [Col 1:16]. Even Satan admits this. Again, he only admits this because Jesus, who claimed to be the Son of God should certainly know that His Father [God] gave Satan this assignment. Again, Satan is only reminding Jesus of this for only one purpose: deception. A lie stands alone, only on one leg. Once you mix it with a little truth then you give that lie "a kick-stander (another leg to stand on). Keep in mind this is not a true leg; it's only a kick-stander.

Satan was correct. Can you believe it? His kingdoms were delivered to him by God. This truth substantiated Satan's claim. Now that Satan's claim has been validated, his appeal to Jesus was to become more appealing. It didn't work. Satan thought he would convince Jesus with natural blessings in exchange for spiritual fulfillment: "worship". This would create the ultimate form of defiance to God. The thought of God's Son worshipping Satan would be a clear example of gaining the world and losing His soul.

Satan was also correct when he told Eve that she would become as "gods," knowing good and evil. Later in Genesis 3:22 God said, "Man has become as one of us, knowing good and evil." Satan is known for mixing the truth with a lie. The best form of deception is when an element of truth is mixed into it.

What Satan didn't know was Jesus's name was already on the title of Earth. He created Heaven and Earth. All things were made by Him, and without Him was not anything made that was made (Jn 1:3; Col 1:16). The Earth is the Lord's and the fullness thereof (Ps 24:1). Satan may "supervise" over this earth, but Jesus is the Landlord. Despite all the negativity you may hear about the craziness going on this earth, God's remnant is the glue that is holding all of this together. Satan has "some" power, but our Lord has <u>All Power</u>!

And the devil said unto him, All this power will I give thee, and the glory of them: for that is delivered unto me; and to whomsoever I will I give it. If thou therefore wilt worship me, all shall be thine. And Jesus answered and said unto him, Get thee behind me, Satan: for it is

written, Thou shalt worship the Lord thy God, and him only shalt thou serve.   (Luke 4:6-8)

Thus saith the LORD; I am returned unto Zion, and will dwell in the midst of Jerusalem: and Jerusalem shall be called a city of truth; and the mountain of the LORD of hosts the holy mountain.   (Zechariah 8:3)

But every man is tempted, when he is drawn away of his own lust, and enticed. Then when lust hath conceived, it bringeth forth sin: and sin, when it is finished, bringeth forth death.   (James 1:14-16)

And so it is written, The first man Adam was made a living soul; the last Adam was made a quickening spirit. The first man is of the earth, earthy: the second man is the Lord from heaven.   (1 Corinthians 15:45, 47)

Watch and pray, that ye enter not into temptation: the spirit indeed is willing, but the flesh is weak.   (Matthew 26:41)

Walk in the Spirit, and ye shall not fulfil the lust of the flesh. For the flesh lusteth against the Spirit, and the Spirit against the flesh: and these are contrary the one to the other: so that ye cannot do the things that ye would.   (Galatians 5:16-17)

For he shall give his angels charge over thee, to keep thee in all thy ways.   (Psalm 91:11-12)

They shall bear thee up in their hands, lest thou dash thy foot against a stone.   (Matthews 4:6)

Now the serpent was more subtle than any beast of the field which the LORD God had made. And he said unto the woman, Yea, hath God said, Ye shall not eat of every tree of the garden?   (Genesis 3:1)

For by him were all things created, that are in heaven, and that are in earth, visible and invisible, whether they be thrones, or dominions, or principalities, or powers: all things were created by him, and for him. *(Colossians 1:16)*

All things were made by him; and without him was not anything made that was made! *(John 1:3)*

The earth is the LORD'S, and the fulness thereof; the world, and they that dwell therein! *(Psalm 24:1)*

How art thou fallen from the Heaven, O Lucifer... *(Isaiah 14:12)*

And He (Jesus) said unto them, "I beheld Satan as lightning fall from Heaven. *(Luke 10:18)*

CHAPTER 6
FATHER : SON

Without controversy, that is without argument or any shadow of doubt, God was manifested in the flesh and dwelt among us (1Tim 3:16). In this book, the words Jesus and God are used interchangeably. Why? Because they are one and the same! Jesus said, "If you've seen me, you've seen the Father; Me and my Father are one" (Jn 10:30).

Today, all believers are considered to be "Israel" [Gods' chosen] spiritually. His chosen people includes everyone that believes on Him and His Son Jesus. The Bible says, "As many as received him, to them gave he power to become the sons of God, even to them that believe on his name" (Jn 1:12). God offers His power to all believers. He offers His inheritance to all believers...to become sons (heirs) of God. The Lord says we are more blessed than Israel because we believe in him; and yet, have not seen him (Jn 20:29). The Israel of old saw Jesus. They walked with Jesus; they talked with Jesus, but many did not believe He was the Son of God (and still don't).

The Bible makes it perfectly clear that Jesus and His Father are One! This may be difficult to perceive for some; however, once you completely understand who God is and the magnitude of His power you will stop trying to figure Him out, and just believe Him at His word. His ways are beyond finding out (Rom 11:33).

Basically speaking, God tells us through Elijah that if you don't want to follow me and serve me then you can go to Hell! (That's the only other alternative.) Our loving God says, "follow Him, or follow Baal." Now somebody tell me, where is Baal going to lead you? God is <u>not</u> instructing us to "go to Hell," as many people misuse this phrase. He is longsuffering toward us hoping that none will be lost, and all men will be saved (2Pet 3:9). He's simply offering you an opportunity of a lifetime: Heaven! He is saying that the only other alternative is Hell. The Lord says, "where I am, you shall be also" (Jn 14:3). However, if you choose to follow the alternative, Baal, he is going to lead you to his domain; Hell.

We only have two choices. Some people deny the existence of both Heaven and Hell. They think it's all over when we die. They think after you die you will go nowhere. If you do the math you find "nowhere" takes Heaven out of the equation. If you think that after you leave here you're going "nowhere" then you have no incentive to pursue Heaven. By seeking first the kingdom of God and His righteousness, we are putting Heaven back into the equation. Without Heaven as an option, your only two choices become Hell and the grave (nothing / nowhere). This kind of math does not add up to anything good. Why would you take Heaven out of any equation? Is it because, you don't believe in the death, burial and resurrection of Christ...or you refuse to believe? If Heaven was never promised to me, neither God's promise that we'll live eternally, it's been worth just having the Lord in my life because I was living in a world of darkness and the Lord brought me the light.

Because, everything God made was good; evil was created by default (Isa 45:7). Anything that is "not good" was "evil!" Even Satan, in his original state, was created good. When God finished creation he looked it over and saw everything that he made and said to Himself "Behold, it is very good" (Gen 1:31). Even Satan! Remember, God told Satan, "Thou was perfect in the day of thy creation...until iniquity [wickedness] was found in you (Ezekiel 28:15). (See Chapter 1)

SON OF GOD

Because of God's enduring love for us, He came down in the form of a man named "Jesus." He decided to personally make an appearance Himself. Because of the magnitude of His being, it would be impossible nor feasible to fit all of God into one man. He's too big. Even if he could or would do it this would limit God because man is limited. He would no longer be Omnipresent (in all places) (Psa 139:7). If God were to put all of His entire being into one man, man would explode. God is just too big.

There are two reasons why Jesus was labeled as the Son of God: (1) God is the Father and Creator of all. Everybody else is His son. This includes you and me and all who believe on His name. (2) It was God who impregnated Mary; not her husband Joseph. Joseph was not Jesus's natural father. God was Jesus' natural father therefore making Jesus, God's Son.

After God created Adam; everybody created after Adam was considered "the son of man," [mankind]. Adam could have been classified as the son of God because Adam was created directly from the hand God. God was his natural Father/Creator. God created Adam first. This why the Bible refers to him as "the first Adam" and Jesus as "the last Adam" (1Cor 15:45). Both were created directly from the hands of God. These were the only two people that God created by His own hands. Adam was created in the very image of God; from the dust of the earth. It would sound good to say that Jesus was created from the dust of Heaven (angel dust) but it really goes deeper than that. Jesus (the Lamb) was slain before "the foundation of the world" (Rev 13:8). This makes God the only father who had a son that died before he was born. (That's another sermon).

The only person that existed before the foundation of the world was God. Jesus was with God. In the beginning was the Word, and the Word was with God; and the word was God (Jn 1:1). The Word was made flesh and dwelt among us. (Jn 1:14). There are only two conclusions we can draw from this information: (1) God was either impregnated with Jesus, and He impregnated Mary, thus making God the Father of Jesus, or (2) God took a portion of Himself and impregnated Mary with a son. Both conclusions make God the Father of Jesus. Since God took a portion of "Himself" and impregnated Mary, the end result would produce a smaller version of "Himself"; thus making that which was "spiritual"; natural. God is a Spirit. If that which is spiritual [God], is made natural [flesh]; then why would that which has now become natural, not be the same? Who else could do something like this; but God? In order to relate to man better; He made himself in the likeness of man, and was found fashioned as a man. Thus making God yet the Father; and through the channels of this immaculate conception in which He and only Him could orchestrate; to also become the Son...! God; then sent an angel (Gabriel) down to Mary's house to instruct her, to name her son "Jesus". Doesn't that sound like a Father? God took the honor and privilege of naming his own Son! In this naming process; the angel fulfilled the prophecy of the prophet Isaiah, to call the child's name "Immanuel", which is interpreted as "God with us" (Matt 1:23, Isa 7:14).

Finally, again God is so big that there is no way His entire being can fit into one human body. By creating Heaven and Earth proves He's bigger than Heaven and earth. God is so Omnipotent ("all" power) and Omniscient ("all" knowing) that 100 percent of God, yet remained in Heaven while 100 percent of Jesus walked this earth (Rev 19:6). In my opinion only 99.9 percent of Gods' omniscience [knowledge] rested in Jesus. Why do I say 99.9 percent? The Scriptures refer to Jesus saying on occasion that certain things were not revealed unto Him but only His father in Heaven knows (Mk 13:32). Time will not allow me to elaborate on that in this book. That is an observation for another book. However, I will leave you with this; while Jesus only obtained 99.9 percent of Gods' omniscience, He was 100 percent human and 100 percent divine.

PROBLEMS?

Problems are a part of life. We must do everything in our power to minimize the ones we bring on ourselves. Jesus told his disciples more than once that "in this world we shall have tribulations, but be of good cheer for I [Jesus] have overcome the world" (St John 16:33). He warns us that "offences will come" (Luke 17:1). He did not say offences "might" come, but that they "will come". Offences are a part of life. Once we understand this, then we can brace ourselves for best / worst offences. The best preparation for this, is to have a consistent prayer life to the only one who can protect us from all harm: the Son of God! He said "I will never leave you nor forsake you" (Hebrews 13:5). If you are a sincere follower, remember "All that ... live godly in Christ Jesus shall suffer persecution (2 Tim 3:12). The Lord may not move the many mountains in your life; but He will give you the strength to climb 'em. "How do I know this?" I've tried everything. Everything else failed me. So one day I decided to "Try The Lord" [Jesus Christ]. Why Don't You Try The Lord? If you don't like him; the devil will be glad to take you back!

Because thou hast seen me, thou hast believed: blessed are they that have not seen, and yet have believed (John 20:29)

And without controversy great is the mystery of godliness: God was manifest in the flesh, justified in the Spirit, seen of angels, preached unto the Gentiles, believed on in the world, received up into glory. (1 Timothy 3:16)

Philip saith unto him, Lord, shew us the Father, and it sufficeth us. (John 14:8)

Jesus saith unto him, ... he that hath seen me hath seen the Father; and how sayest thou then, Shew us the Father? (John 14:9)

I and my Father are one. (John 10:30)

O... how unsearchable are his judgments, and his ways past finding out! (Romans 11:33)

And if I go and prepare a place for you, I will come again, and receive you unto myself; that where I am, there ye may be also. (John 14:3)

And God saw everything that he had made, and, behold, it was very good! (Genesis 1:31)

...the Lamb slain from the foundation of the world. (Revelation 13:8)

In the beginning was the Word, and the Word was with God, and the Word was God. (John 1:1)

And the Word was made flesh, and dwelt among us! (John 1:14)

Behold, a virgin shall be with child, and shall bring forth a son, and they shall call his name Emmanuel, which being interpreted is, God with us. (Matthew 1:23)

PROBLEMS?

Therefore the Lord himself shall give you a sign; Behold, a virgin shall conceive, and bear a son, and shall call his name Immanuel.   (Isaiah 7:14)

...Alleluia: for the Lord God "Omnipotent" reigns..
(Revelation 19:6)

But of that day and that hour knoweth no man, no, not the angels which are in Heaven, neither the Son, but the Father.   (Mark 13:32)

God is a Spirit: and they that worship him must worship him in spirit and in truth.   (John 4:24)

.... and was made in the likeness of men: And being found in fashion as a man, he humbled himself, and became obedient unto death, even the death of the cross.
(Philippians 2:7,8)

ABOUT THE AUTHOR:

Terry Matthews is the Pastor and founder of Crown of Life Ministries in Bakersfield, California since 1991. He was born in Flint, Michigan, during the time of the Alabama bus boycott inspired by the infamous Rosa Parks. He has seen more than his share of injustice during his lifetime. He knew at a very early age that the only real protection he could count on was the Lord during turbulent times. He is the last of eleven children. He served in the U.S. Army for a short time immediately following the Vietnam War. He recorded one gospel album, "Why Don't You Try The Lord". He received his call to the ministry in 1983. He moved to Bakersfield in 1984. He held a prison ministry in California for seven years which included the two Chowchilla State prisons and Tehachapi State Prison to name a few. In 2019 he returned back into the prison ministry again. The prison ministry and the writing of this book is a small attempt to honor the commission of Jesus, according to Mark 16:15; "Go into all the world and preach the gospel to all of Gods' creation".

Booking Information:

Web Site: www.crownoflifeministriesca.com
Email: info@crownoflifeministriesca.com

Location:

Crown of Life Ministries CA
1100 Gorrill Street
Bakersfield, California 93307

Mailing Address:

Crown of Life Ministries
P.O. Box 70964
Bakersfield, CA 93387

www.ingramcontent.com/pod-product-compliance
Ingram Content Group UK Ltd.
Pitfield, Milton Keynes, MK11 3LW, UK
UKHW022220230426
12048UKWH00016BA/958